3. The entire world.

Sousa's band was popular not only in the United States, but all over the world! Sousa and his band played for thousands of people everywhere, including South Africa, Europe, Australia, New Zealand, Cuba, Canada, the Fiji Islands, the Hawaiian Islands, and many other places.

MAP OF THE ENTIRE TOTAL COMPLETE WORLD

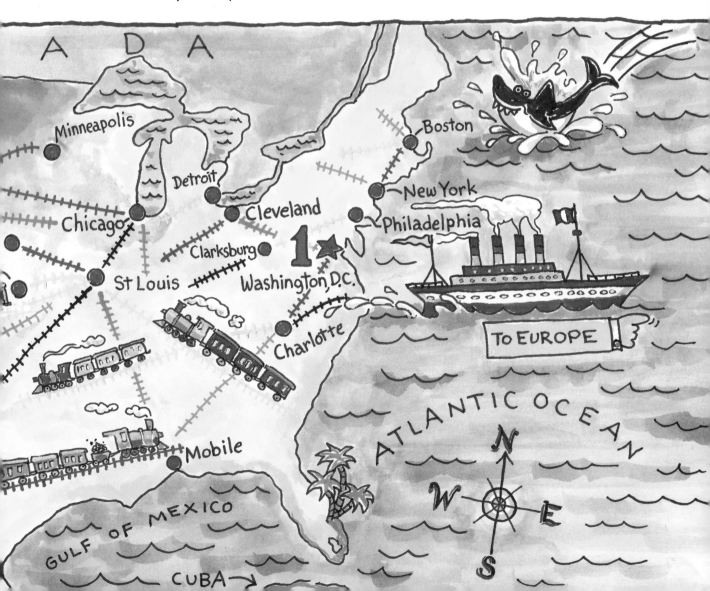

TIMELINE OF JOHN PHILIP SOUSA'S LIFE

1854 John Philip Sousa is born in Washington, D.C.

1861 Sousa begins music lessons with a local teacher. Over the next few years, he studies singing, violin, piano, flute, cornet, and trombone.

1865 At age eleven, John Philip forms his own dance orchestra! He leads seven adult musicians.

1868 Sousa enlists as an apprentice in the U.S. Marine Corps as a member of the Marine Band.

1874 -1879 John Philip is honorably discharged from the Marines. He starts working as a musician, conducting and playing in an opera house, a roadshow band, and a theater orchestra. He meets and marries Jane Bellis.

1880 Sousa enlists again in the Marines. This time, however, he is leader of the Marine Band.

 THIS WAY

 UP HERE

1882 Sousa's first published operetta, *The Smugglers*, is performed.

1891 Sousa takes the U.S. Marine Band on its first tour across the United States.

1892 John Philip Sousa leaves the Marines and starts his own band.

1896 Sousa writes *The Stars and Stripes Forever*, his most famous piece.

1900 The Sousa Band travels to Europe for the first time.

1910 The band begins a long overseas tour. They play for huge crowds in countries all over the world.

1917 At the age of sixty-two, John Philip Sousa enlists in the U.S. Navy! He forms a 300-piece band at the Great Lakes Naval Training Center near Chicago.

1929 Sousa's first radio concert is broadcast all over the country.

1932 After rehearsing for a concert in Reading, Pennsylvania, John Philip Sousa becomes ill. He dies of a heart attack only a few hours later.

GETTING TO KNOW
THE WORLD'S
GREATEST COMPOSERS

JOHN PHILIP
SOUSA

WRITTEN AND ILLUSTRATED BY MIKE VENEZIA

CONSULTANT
DONALD FREUND, PROFESSOR OF COMPOSITION,
INDIANA UNIVERSITY SCHOOL OF MUSIC

CHILDREN'S PRESS®

An Imprint of Scholastic Inc.

For my editor, Shari Joffe—thanks for all your support.

Picture Acknowledgements
Photographs ©: cover and title page: Stock Montage; 3: Library of Congress; 6: 1896 by the John Church Company/Ssilvers/Wikimedia; 7 top left: Sheridan Libraries/Levy/Gado/Getty Images; 7 top right: John Church Co., Cincinnati, 1907/Library of Congress; 7 bottom: Sam Fox Publishing Co., Cleveland, 1922/Library of Congress; 10: United States Marine Band; 11: Universal History Archive/Getty Images; 12: United States Marine Band; 17: Library of Congress; 18, 20, 22-23, 25, 30 right: United States Marine Band; 30 left: Library of Congress; 32: Bain News Service/Library of Congress.

Library of Congress Cataloging-in-Publication Data

Names: Venezia, Mike, author, illustrator.
Title: John Philip Sousa / written and illustrated by Mike Venezia ;
    consultant, Donald Freund.
Description: Revised edition. | New York, NY : Children's Press, 2018. |
    Series: Getting to know the world's greatest composers | Includes
    bibliographical references and index.
Identifiers: LCCN 2017048075| ISBN 9780531228692 (library binding : alk.
    paper) | ISBN 9780531233726 (pbk. : alk. paper)
Subjects: LCSH: Sousa, John Philip, 1854-1932--Juvenile literature. |
    Composers--United States--Biography--Juvenile literature
Classification: LCC ML3930.S7 V46 2018 | DDC 784.8/4092 [B] --dc23 LC record available at
https://lccn.loc.gov/2017048075

Scholastic Inc., 557 Broadway, New York, NY 10012.

1 2 3 4 5 6 7 8 9 10 R 27 26 25 24 23 22 21 20 19 18

American composer John Philip Sousa was known as the March King.

John Philip Sousa was born in Washington, D.C., the capital of the United States, in 1854. He always loved his country and showed his love by writing some of the most original and patriotic music ever.

John Philip Sousa is best known for his thrilling marches. The unusual titles he gave them may be unfamiliar to some people today. But almost everyone has heard *El Capitan*, *The Washington Post*, *High School Cadets*, *Manhattan Beach*, *King Cotton*, and *Semper Fidelis* at one time or another. These marches are always being played in movies, TV shows, parades, and by school bands.

John Philip Sousa said that when he wanted to write a march, he would sometimes try to imagine scenes of battles with rifles firing and cannons exploding. He would hear the clanking of swords and the sound of soldiers marching to the drum beat. All of a sudden, a tune would come to him. He was always amazed how this happened.

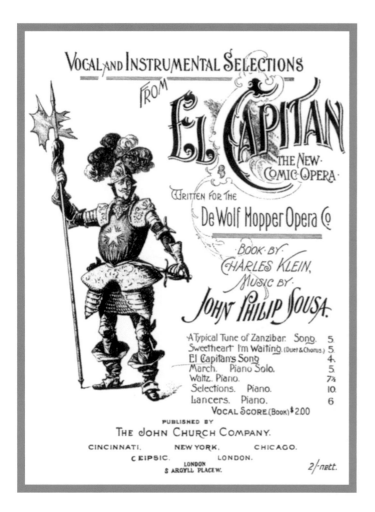

The cover of some sheet music from Sousa's operetta *El Capitan*

Sousa also composed music for operettas. An operetta is a short, usually comic play in which the actors sing and dance their parts as the orchestra plays along. John Philip Sousa was proud of the music he wrote for these plays. He liked some of it better than some of the marches he composed.

Sheet-music covers for three
of Sousa's many marches

John couldn't understand
why his operetta music
never became as
popular as his marches.
It was always a
disappointment
to him.

Before John Philip Sousa was born, the United States didn't really have classical music it could call its own. The United States was a fairly new country, and American composers had not yet become well known.

In big cities, people went to concerts and listened to the works of European composers, like Johann Sebastian Bach, Ludwig van Beethoven, and Wolfgang Amadeus Mozart. Tickets to these concerts were expensive, and people had to dress in fancy clothes to get in. Everyone was pretty

snobby about the whole thing. In the rest of the country, people had to listen to bands and musical entertainers who weren't very good a lot of the time. Everybody wanted to hear music so much, though, that they were happy to accept anything that came along.

While John Philip Sousa was growing up, he was lucky to be able to listen to the many military bands that played in Washington, D.C. At that time, the Civil War was going on. Washington, D.C., was almost like an armed camp and was under attack at times by Confederate soldiers.

The United States Marine Band in the 1860s, during the Civil War

A Civil War battle

Army bands were all over the place. They were needed to announce daily activities or send commands and signals. They were also an important way of keeping soldiers' spirits up during long, boring marches. Sometimes bands would play old, familiar songs that reminded soldiers of happier times. These military bands made a deep impression on John Philip Sousa.

John Philip Sousa's parents

John Philip Sousa grew up in a musical family. His father played the trombone in the United States Marine Band. Mr. Sousa encouraged his son to take violin lessons at an early age. He taught him to play the trombone and other band instruments as well.

Soon John's parents and teachers knew John had a special musical talent. When he was only eleven years old, John put together a dance band that played in the Washington, D.C., area. He was the leader of seven grown men, and the band became pretty popular.

When John Philip Sousa was thirteen years old, the circus came to his town. One night, the owner of the circus heard John's dance band play. He really liked what he heard and asked John if he would like to join the circus and become their band leader.

John Philip Sousa thought traveling around the world with the circus would be a great idea! He decided to join up and run away from home. Fortunately, Mr. Sousa found out about the plan. The next morning, he marched his son down to the marine barracks and signed him up

in the Marine Corps band. At the age of thirteen, John Philip Sousa was a United States Marine. He was also in a place where his father could keep an eye on him.

At that time, the U.S. Marines were very different from the way they are today. Things weren't so strict. In fact, John and other band members could leave at the end of the day and play their instruments at dances or city concerts to make extra money.

John enjoyed his stay in the Marine Band and learned a lot. After seven years, though, he decided to leave. John felt there were musical opportunities outside the Marine Band where he could learn more and develop his talents.

John Philip Sousa as a young man

Jane Bellis Sousa, John Philip Sousa's wife

John Philip Sousa began traveling to different cities where he played his violin and composed music. In one city, he met and fell in love with a singer from a theater group. Her name was Jane Bellis. John and Jane got married and soon after their wedding, an important thing happened. John was asked to come back to the U.S. Marine Band. This time, though, it was not as a musician, but as their leader! John was glad to accept the job.

When John got back to Washington, D.C.,
however, he was disappointed to find the
band in pretty bad shape. Many of the band
members really didn't want to be there
anymore. Their uniforms were worn out
and the music they played seemed old and
boring to John.

The front cover of a concert program for the first national concert tour by the U.S. Marine Band

John got to work right away. He decided to try to make this band the best military band in the world. He started by getting new and better musicians to join up, and he made them practice for long hours. He got rid of a lot of the dull music the band was used to playing, and replaced it with more modern music by European and American composers. John added his own marches, too.

One of John's favorite assignments was to play for the president of the United States whenever he needed music for a party or special government affair.

John Philip Sousa got to meet five different presidents during the time he was the leader of the Marine Band. During this time, he also wrote some of his best marches, including *Semper Fidelis* and *The Washington Post*. He even became known as the March King.

The U.S. Marine Band became more popular than ever before. Sometimes thousands of

people would gather for its concerts. One day after a concert, a businessman named David Blakely talked to John Philip Sousa about starting up his own band. John liked the idea. He thought that if he had his own band, he could travel more and play his great music for people all over the United States, or even all over the world. He could choose all his favorite pieces to play and make a lot more money, too. In 1892, he left the marines to start his very own band.

The U.S. Marine Band as led by John Philip Sousa (center)

After twelve years of leading the U.S. Marine Band, John Philip Sousa knew exactly how to put a successful band together. He started by hiring the best musicians he could find. He spent weeks rehearsing and training them. He made sure they had the coolest-looking uniforms, too. John knew his band would have to look great as well as sound great.

David Blakely became John's partner and manager. He made sure the band was set up to play in different cities and took care of advertising.

When John was done putting the band together, it turned out to be a combination symphony orchestra and concert band. Sousa's band hardly ever marched, but they could play any type of music, from simple American folk songs to big, famous symphonies.

John Philip Sousa formed his own concert band in 1892.

From the very beginning, John Philip Sousa's band was a big hit! He always made sure he played music that everyone could enjoy.

John and his band traveled to as many cities and towns as possible. It was almost like a big holiday when they came to town. Schools and businesses closed, and everyone from miles around would go to the concert. Sometimes the audience loved the music so much that they demanded the band play their favorite piece over and over again. John Philip Sousa never minded doing this, especially if they wanted to hear one of his marches.

John Philip Sousa's marches were and still are popular all over the world. The idea for his most famous march, *The Stars and Stripes Forever*, came to him while he was traveling on an ocean liner in 1896. Later, John remembered how clearly he had heard an imaginary band play *The Stars and Stripes Forever* in his head as

the rough sea bounced his ship back and forth. John believed this piece was inspired by God. As soon as he got home, he wrote the notes down exactly as he heard them. The powerful rhythms of this patriotic march have made people so proud of being American that they often stand while this song is being played.

The Stars and Stripes Forever did just what John Philip Sousa thought a good march should do, which was make goosebumps chase each other up and down your back when you listen to it. Even when his band played *The Stars and Stripes Forever* in other countries, it gave people the same kind of proud feeling as it did in the United States.

For many years, John Philip Sousa and his band were among the most famous entertainers in the world. Wherever John went, kings, queens, presidents, and mayors of towns honored him. John was given so many medals, he could never wear them all at the same time.

John Philip Sousa leading
a naval marching band
during World War I

John Philip Sousa lived to be seventy-seven years old. During a time when radio and television were not yet around, he made it possible for thousands of people all over to hear good music. He helped show how important American composers were by playing their compositions in different countries around the world. He always had fun playing music, but treated each musical piece as if it were the most important one ever, whether it was a simple street tune or a great symphony.

LEARN MORE BY TAKING THE SOUSA QUIZ!

(ANSWERS ON THE NEXT PAGE.)

1. TRUE OR FALSE:
As a child, John Philip Sousa was in poor health much of the time. When he grew up, he was too weak to play sports or enjoy any physical activities.

2. Sousa was the leader of the U.S. Marine Band long enough to serve under five American presidents. Who were they?

a Franklin Pierce, James Buchanan, Abe Lincoln, Andrew Johnson, Ulysses S. Grant

b Rutherford Hayes, James Garfield, Chester A. Arthur, Grover Cleveland, Benjamin Harrison

c Harry Truman, Dwight Eisenhower, John Kennedy, Lyndon Johnson, Richard Nixon

3. John Philip Sousa loved food and enjoyed cooking. His favorite main-course recipe was once printed in a Chicago newspaper. What was Sousa's favorite meal?

a Chicago style deep-dish pizza

b Veggie burritos

c Spaghetti and meatballs

4. After an exhausting nonstop concert tour, Sousa's doctor suggested he and Mrs. Sousa take a relaxing ocean voyage. The trip was a flop, and anything but relaxing! What was the reason for the Sousas' horrible voyage?

a The ship was attacked by a giant squid.

b The shuffleboard tournament was cancelled due to nonstop rain.

c A slow-burning fire broke out and was ready to burst into flames at any moment.

5. TRUE OR FALSE:
John Philip Sousa was America's first recording star.

ANSWERS

1. **FALSE** John Philip Sousa was actually a sporting powerhouse! He loved playing baseball and was into sailing, bicycling, boxing, swimming, horseback riding, hunting, and fishing. He was an expert in a type of target shooting competition called trapshooting. Sousa is considered one of the greatest trap shooters in the game's history!

2. **b** John Philip Sousa didn't just play music at presidential events, he got to know the five presidents he served under pretty well, too.

3. **c** Sousa's recipe for spaghetti and meatballs was published in the *Chicago Herald* newspaper in 1916. He said the recipe served from 6 to 8 people, and it was his favorite dish.

4. **c** Not only were there rough seas and storms during the Sousas' "relaxing" voyage, but the ship caught on fire! Smoke was everywhere! Fortunately, the ship's crew was able to keep the fire under control for the next few days and everyone was able to disembark safely.

5. **TRUE** Even though John Philip Sousa hated the sound of recorded music at the time, he eventually agreed to have his music recorded. He realized that it would be a good way for people all over the United States to hear his marches, operas, and songs. Sousa's recordings became hugely popular, which made him America's first big recording star.